THE ROMAN WEST

AND

THE BYZANTINE EAST

by

Bishop Chrysostomos of Oreoi
and
Hieromonk Auxentios

CENTER FOR TRADITIONALIST ORTHODOX STUDIES

Etna, California 96027-0398

Portions of this book appeared in
Orthodoxy and Papism
by Bishop Chrysostomos
(C.T.O.S., 1983)

Library of Congress Catalog Card Number
88-70893

ISBN 0-911165-12-6

ABOUT THE AUTHORS

The Rt. Rev. Chrysostomos is Titular Bishop of Oreoi (Greece) and Exarch in America for the Synod of Old Calendar Greek Orthodox Bishops under Metropolitan Cyprian of Oropos and Fili. Educated at the University of California and Princeton University, he has taught at Princeton, the University of California, Ashland College, the Ashland Theological Seminary, and, as a Visiting Professor, at the Theological Institute of Uppsala University in Sweden. He has been a Marsden Research Fellow at Oxford University and at the Center for Traditionalist Orthodox Studies, a National Endowment for the Humanities Fellow, and a Visiting Scholar at the Harvard Divinity School. Bishop Chrysostomos is the author of numerous books in Orthodox theology and related topics, and has authored almost fifty scholarly papers in Byzantine history, Orthodox theological studies, and experimental psychology. His Grace is an Old Calendar zealot and an active advocate of inter-jurisdictional dialogue among the Orthodox Churches in America.

The Reverend Hieromonk Auxentios is Steward of the St. Gregory Palamas Monastery. A graduate of Princeton University, where he studied with the renowned Orthodox theologian, the late Protopresbyter Georges Florovsky, Father Auxentios completed his Licentiate in Orthodox Theological Studies at the C.T.O.S. Presently a doctoral student in Liturgics at the Graduate Theological Union, Berkeley, he is the author of numerous scholarly papers and several books in Orthodox theology.

TABLE OF CONTENTS

INTRODUCTION

This book is a revision and amplification of the introductory chapter in a book published by the first author (Bishop Chrysostomos —then an Archimandrite and Abbot of the St. Gregory Palamas Monastery) in 1983: *Orthodoxy and Papism*. That book, now out of print, contained, in addition to a comparative treatment of Eastern and Western Christian traditions from an historiographical and comparative theological perspective, a translation of Photios Kontoglou's famous commentary on Orthodoxy and the Latin Church, "What Orthodoxy is and What Papism Is." Both authors have worked carefully to preserve, in this separate work, the spirit of Kontoglou's uncompromising and critical approach to the relationship between Orthodoxy and Latin Christianity, but in the present volume without some of the terse language so characteristic of the inimitable style of this great and memorable man of latters and champion of the Greek Orthodox Faith.

Many Orthodox Christians living in the West have a truncated and distorted view of the history of their Church. This is partly because many of the Orthodox in Western Europe and the Americas come from a Greek Catholic background, having entered into the Orthodox Church as part of the massive return of Slavic Uniates from Rome following the communist revolutions in Eastern Europe earlier this century. One Orthodox jurisdictions in the United States, the Orthodox Church in America, is still largely a Church of believers whose forebears were a generation ago attached to the Roman Unia —a fact almost forgotten among its present Faithful. The bulk of these former Uniates are still very much the captives of historiographies, theologies, and customs imposed upon them by their Latinized ancestors. Their struggle for Orthodoxy —though there are among them, fortunately, some with deep roots in the Orthodox ethos— is part of a yet unfinished struggle for a genuine Orthodox identity.

At the same time, the ecumenical movement has taken its toll on the Orthodox Church. Doing so in a spirit which engenders and demands respect and love for non-Orthodox Christians —the kind of love that one would expect from a mother—, the Orthodox Church claims to represent the Church established by Christ, to be the very continuation of that Church in present times, and to be the repository of all "that the Lord gave, the Apostles preached, and the Fathers preserved," as one Church Father puts it. This vision is at odds with the "ecclesiology" of contemporary ecumenism, which is no longer so much a movement that would guarantee the Orthodox to believe as they do, but one which would demand of Orthodoxy loyalty to an ecclesiological relativism. This demand has caused many Orthodox to capitulate to a view of the Church which constitutes virtual spiritual self-abnegation. And in this capitulation, some Orthodox Churches have failed to teach their Faithful what it means to be Orthodox: what it means to be preservers of the "criterion" of Truth, the Mother Church of Christianity.

The purpose of the present book, then, is to provide a sharp contrast —perhaps a bit too sharp at times— between the Roman West and the Byzantine East, between the Church of Rome and the Eastern Orthodox Churches from which the Roman Catholic Church emerged and to which it was once so closely bound as a Church of Orthodox Martyrs, Saints, and

Hierarchs. The Orthodox Christian who thinks that he is an "Eastern Catholic," who belongs to a Church that differs from the Church of Rome only by virtue of its married clergy and an "Eastern Pope" in Constantinople, will be shocked by what he reads in these pages. For, indeed, the Eastern and Western Churches are still as far from one another as the East is from the West. And if this separation is lamentable, knowing about it is the surest path to reunion. Reunion wrought by misunderstanding and ignorance is false reunion and is a violation of the spirit of Christianity —as witnessed by the False Union of Florence (a reunion imposed on the Orthodox by force and with a spirit which should embarrass the West) and by other such superficial efforts at the political, rather than spiritual, reconciliation of the Eastern and Western Churches.

The West has gained ascendency. Its distortions of history have prevailed. Political ecumenism, a Western disease that infected the Eastern Church at the beginning of this century, has helped to perpetuate these distortions. Some Westerners, then, feeling their power and guarding the prerogatives of cultural and political ascendency, will find much of what we write in this book insulting. We believe that others, however, will understand that things spiritual rest on the sharp edge of truth, which divides away both arrogance and power. Westerner or Easterner, a stark contrast of two differing traditions is something that can aid any Christian in understanding who he is and what must be done in discovering that ultimate truth which unites all of us, despite our divisions — which, honestly understood, gives our very divisions meaning!

The Authors

dates, and the antecedents that we assume for events —these things are our concern. These are the "facts," the data, the pieces that make up our view of the world in which our theologies and Christian values are formed. These are the things that tell us, not what we believe, but why we believe what we do here and now.

All history, one might say, is artificial. It would be, in fact, almost trite to argue that history is a lie. The argument is just too obvious. Any time that we recount what is not present to us, we are simply fabricating a probable picture of the past. This can never be objective. The Western view of the Christian past, however, is particularly artificial —it is a rather "whopping lie," as the modern idiom would have it, if only because it ignores the historical experience of more than half of the Christian world, the Christian East, from which Western Christianity itself ultimately derives! Yet, it has gained such ascendancy that one is hesitant to challenge it. It is so ubiquitous that even Eastern Christians, especially those living in the West, often embrace it themselves. And if they do not, in fact, embrace it as their personal view, they often feel compelled to speak within its framework in trying to present their own perspectives on the Christian past. The Western view has, indeed, become triumphant, despite its inadequacies in accounting, as we shall see, for a vast part of Christian history.

What is the Western view of the Christian past? It is largely a Roman Catholic view (and one which fits, we might add, by certain adaptations, the historiography of the Protestant world.) It begins by assuming that the Christian era was initiated in a small outpost of the Roman Empire by Jesus of Nazareth, a Palestinian. Jesus Christ, the promised Messiah of

Chapter I

HISTORIOGRAPHY AND THE
CHRISTIAN CHURCH

The Eastern and Western Views

In every culture, individuals have some notion of their past, whether this notion is conveyed in legends and myths, or in some chronological presentation of happenings and events. All of us live with these ideas about where we come from and what things in the past have formed us as we are in the present. The Christian, too, has a notion of the past, and it is conveyed to him in hagiography and Biblical parables (legends and myths), as well as in chronologies, or historical accounts as we commonly understand them today. As for the legends and myths, these belong to our theological heritage; they are part of the "truths" that are meta-historical, that convey to us the essence of our Faith. (We might note that one must not understand the notions of "legend" and "myth" as they are popularly understood. Legends and myths are styles in which events are recounted, emphasizing, more than data about time, the eternal and philosophical importance of events that just happen to occur at this or that time. In other words, legends and myths are by no means descriptions of nonexistent events, but are simply special ways of speaking about events —in a manner that rises above history.) These we need not touch upon here. But the chronologies, the way that we arrange

the Jews and the revelation in the flesh of God Himself, spread His message throughout the borders of
his small Jewish nation, appointing, among his fo-
lowers, Apostles to spread the message of Christianity throughout the world. After Christ's death and
Resurrection, the Christian message was indeed
spread throughout the Mediterranean world —the
known world. Its bold theology earned its adherents
martyr's crowns in all parts of the Empire, but especially in Rome, the capital, where many Christians
were taken to be executed in the public games. The
Church of Rome, gaining eminence not only
through the witness of the martyrs in the arena, but
through the person of its founders, Sts. Peter and
Paul (though primarily through St. Peter, the "Prince
of the Apostles"), soon became the most important
center of Christianity.

As Christianity became centered in the capital of
the Empire, it gained more and more attention from
the imperial authorities. This resulted, at first, in
greater persecution. But later, as the power of the
Christian witness grew, the imperial authorities
themselves succumbed to the Christian religion.
Year by year, Christianity became more powerful, until finally, in the fourth century, it was declared the
official religion of the Roman Empire, under the Emperor Constantine. Though a nominal Christian, the
Emperor took part in theological debates and dialogues, helping form and direct Christian dogma, so
that the stability of the Church might be guaranteed.
Christianity, becoming part of the Empire, soon developed a strong external structure and placed itself
under the manifest leadership of the Bishop of
Rome, who presided over the most important
Church in the Empire and who was a successor of the
Prince of the Apostles. While the Emperor Constan-

tine had moved the political capital of the Empire to the ancient city of Byzantium in the East (renaming it, after himself, Constantinople), the seat of the power of the Church rested in the See of Rome.

In the fifth century, with the incursions of Germanic barbarians into the Empire eventually reaching Rome itself, the Roman Empire fell. Its power base shattered, it entered into an age of decline, in which Christianity became the mortar which held together the structure of society. The Bishop of Rome, head of the Church, began to assume the direction of man's temporal and spiritual life, since the temporal authorities of the world had become virtually ineffective. Seeing the turmoil of the world, many Christians retreated to the deserts as monastics, fearing that the apocalyptic age was upon them. Society, demoralized and shaken to its foundations, found strength only in the power of the Church, the surety of the Christian promise of a better life in the "other world," and the paternal guidance of Christ's vicar on earth, the Roman Pontiff.

Into this darkness, according to the popular Western narrative of the rise of Christianity, the ninth century brought a glimmer of hope and renaissance of sorts: the Holy Roman Empire. From among the German tribes, a Roman Empire was being reborn, with the hand of the Bishop of Rome guiding the course of this new secular power. At the death of the Emperor Constantine — as a rather strikingly bogus piece of history would have it—, the temporal power of the Roman Empire passed on to the Bishop of Rome, as though in anticipation of the chaos that was to follow the Emperor's death. With the crowning of Charlemagne on Christmas Day, 800, the Pope of Rome finally put this power to use. At long last, after years of social decline, the manifest authority of the Papacy had come to be expressed in the reborn political wing of the Holy Roman Empire. The Church emerged from its burdensome role as the overseer of both Church and State, delegating its secular power to a new Emperor.

The renaissance of the Carolingian period was short-lived. The Holy Roman Empire went on its course, as Church and State began to vie for power, the Emperor making sole claim to authority in the Empire, the Bishop of Rome asserting his privilege of bestowing such power on the Emperor by virtue of the authority of the Pontiff over the Church *and* State. The rivalries that ensued, in the midst of famine and plagues, we normally call the Middle Ages, or, to the less objective observers of history, the "Dark Ages" (in fact, these are years of rich social and cultural growth in the West). These are the years of the powerful Church, dominated by the Pope, constantly in conflict with the State. And it was during these years (in 1054, to be specific) that a number of Eastern Christians, claiming that their own Pope, or Patriarch [in the Early Church the term "Pope" applied to all of the Bishops of the more famous Sees and was used much in the same way that we use the term "Patriarch" today], in Constantinople held authority over the Empire, broke from the Roman Catholic Church and established the Eastern Orthodox Church. They united under themselves most of the Christians of Eastern Europe (Russia, Bulgaria, and so on) and the Levant.

With the end of the fourteenth century, the years of supposed darkness and Church rule finally came to an end. The Italian city-states envisioned a political power free from the Church, and intellectuals and artists began to free themselves from the concerns of religion. They were free to exalt man, rather than

God, and a "Renaissance" was upon them. The Church attempted to retain its power and to stem the excesses of secularism, but faith in man and his world grew by leaps and bounds. The classical world of art and literature was brought back into human consciousness, and man began to put religion in its proper place, the world in its. A true separation of the spiritual and the mundane was finally taking form. In the shadows of this new dawning of interest in the world for the world's sake, the separated Christians of the East, fearing invasions from their Moslem enemies to the South, attempted a union with the Church of Rome. Their intransigent Eastern ideas, their inarticulate and unsystematic theological notions, and their years of estrangement from the Roman Empire, however, made such a union ultimately impossible. They faded out of Western consciousness, save for the few Byzantines who migrated to the West to peddle their artistic and literary talents and the Russians, who later entered into the Western pale by virtue of an intentional "Westernization" of their culture and religion.

The separation of the political power of the Roman Empire from the supervision of the Papacy, combined with a new faith in human reason and secular knowledge, led to the end of the unity of the Christian Church. Granted, some Eastern Christians had separated from the Church in the fifth century over certain complex and pedantic arguments about the nature of Christ, and in 1054 the "Pope of the East" had led many of its followers into schism, but these were incidents related to unimportant factors in minor outposts of the Empire. It was in the sixteenth century, when the Protestant challenge to the Pope's leadership in the Church, that the *real* unity of the Church was broken. There began, with the famous declarations of Martin Luther, a split in the Christian Church that has persisted to this day. Challenging the historical emergence of the Roman Pontiff as the unifying force in the political and spiritual development of the Roman Empire, the ancient civilized world, the Protestant Reformation came to question, not only the Papacy's authority in mundane matters, but its leadership in matters of the Faith. The ancient Pontiff of the Church, who had gathered Christians, after three hundred years of chaos and persecution, under his wing in the Early Church, who had guided civilized Europe through the dark days of the Middle Ages, was now under attack by his own. The center of Christianity had moved from the Pontiff to the authority of the Bible, the individual Christian conscience, and the body of believers.

And so has the Christian Church remained to this day. Until very recently, the Pontiff held to his ancient claim to primacy over the Church, and the followers of the Reformation held their claims of the primacy of Scripture and Faith. These two antipodes in the development of Christian history, of the Christian Church, it seemed, were forever doomed to challenge one another. With the advent of the ecumenical age, however, there has developed a certain "give and take" among Christians, proponents of the Reformation admitting the historical role of the Bishop of Rome in the formation of the Church, the Papacy admitting to a certain overstatement of its powers in that development. The history of the Christian Church, in a nutshell, has reached this age of rapprochement.

Needless to say, the amateur historian, not to mention the competent historical scholar, would take exception to much of what we have said above.

History is not all that simple. We have lumped hundreds of years of complex history under ridiculously inclusive titles, reducing this complexity to an artificial simplicity. And, of course, history does not take place in concrete cycles or eras. No one woke up some morning in the fifteenth century and declared that the Renaissance had dawned during his night's rest. History develops slowly and without the patterns that we, for convenience, impose on it. What patterns do emerge in the course of time are, for the most part, far more subtle and enigmatic than our historiographical schemes would suggest.

And yet, there is something hauntingly compelling about the historical outline that we have presented. It sounds simple, and we might protest that it is not sophisticated enough; but still, almost any Roman Catholic would think that it rings true. Hardly a single Protestant would find it wholly uncomfortable. In the more honest moments of the simple view of life to which we are almost all at times reduced, this account of the history of the Christian Church seems all too obvious. On it, almost every Roman Catholic (and many a Protestant Christian) would hang his theology. It, too, fits. And if nothing else commends this outline, the vague memories of an introductory college course in Western civilization certainly line up with it and argue for its authenticity.

But this overview of history is, to be sure, a veritable lie. It survives only because it ignores what threatens it. It suffices because it excises all that which compromises it. It is not an encompassing view of history, therefore, and by nature sustains itself by ignorance —by a deliberate ignorance of the Eastern Christian world, indeed by an ignorance of the very birthplace of Christianity, the Levant. It by nature moves away from the first three hundred years of the Christian witness, covering this departure from three centuries of history by the bold assertion that this era was one of chaos and uncertainty. It deliberately relegates some of the most vibrant Christian witnesses to an *ahistorical* realm, making meta-historical that which was the very foundation of the historical Church. And most tragic of all, it dismisses as insignificant the Roman Empire which it so assiduously argues that it represents, casting off the wealth, power, and overwhelming numbers of Christians of the Byzantine Empire as mere footnotes to real history. In the style of the celebrated historian and myopic Westerner, Edward Gibbon, it makes history a much desired and well told fable, but not an honest effort to understand the past. It is an ill-held view of the Christian Church that does little service to the approximation of truth that history, as a recounting of events, must be. And it alienates, in that disservice, the East and West both from one another and from the true meta-historical past that they actually share.

Let us look, then, at a Byzantine view of the history of the Christian Church. And let us see if it is not, in its more expansive scope and in its acknowledgement of the Christian West, a more encompassing view. Let us see if the historiography of the East is not by far more objective. In doing this, we must understand something about the Byzantine mind. Orthodox thinkers have never thought in the Cartesian method of the West. That is, unlike the Western thinker, they do not begin at "zero," at "nothing," and then develop their observations about things; rather, the Byzantines begin at "one," as it were, and work from certain basic assumptions. Therefore, the Western theologian might begin by assuming that

God does not exist (or, indeed, that nothing at all exists), and then proceed to establish the existence of God and the created world. The Eastern theologian, however, always assumes the existence of God and His creation, basing his intellectual observations on this *a priori* assumption. The Byzantine view of history, too, makes certain assumptions about the Christian Church and proceeds from them. These assumptions rather drastically change the way that an Easterner looks at the origins of Christianity.

The Western Christian, we have said, looks at Christianity as a phenomenon that grew up in an isolated part of the Roman Empire and ultimately spread throughout the Mediterranean world. In trying to understand the spread of Christianity, most Western thinkers have therefore tried to understand how an obscure religion in Palestine could have accomplished this triumph. Even if a Westerner acknowledges the divine nature of the Christian religion, he is wont to assume that the Church was something less than a divine manifestation and usually imagines that it took root in the Empire because of certain social, political, and economic factors that favored its growth. An Easterner does not start with this idea, that the Christian Church acted on society and established its divine mission through an historical process. He assumes, rather, that the Church is, in fact, divine and that history is the story of its divine manifestation. In short, the Westerner begins with a secular history that is *infused with a divine witness*, but with a "zero" assumption about the divine *content* of history. The Byzantine begins with a history which is divine, the content of which is the story of the manifestation of the divine. If we can grasp this distinction, we can fully understand an Orthodox view of the Roman Empire into which Christ was born.

For the Byzantine, the birth of Jesus Christ was an event of significance to the known world. His birth fulfilled a promise by God to the Jews that he would reveal Himself in the form of a man, and it fulfilled the longing of the ancient philosophers to find the *Logos*, the divine formula by which the worlds of the flesh and the spirit might be intimately bound. To the Greek philosophers especially, the birth of Christ heralded a manifest knowledge of God, an archetype of the nobler side of man that they had heretofore known only in philosophic theory. The world, then, had been prepared for Christ, and the message of His Resurrection and the spread of His Church were, quite simply, elements in the unfolding of the divine drama which is history. The world had been prepared for Christ in its historical development, not only among the Jews and Greeks, but in the religious longings of all peoples of the world, who pined for a manifestation of what they had so long known and felt in their hearts. Christ was not born in an obscure corner of a social, political, and economic unit called the Roman Empire, but was born into an Empire which was formed by the common desire of all civilized men to know man and to know God.

The pagan society of pre-Christian times, we see, was for the Eastern Orthodox Christian, for the Byzantine, not a godless society into which the divine infused itself. It was a society being prepared for the manifestation of God, being molded by divine forces. The paganism of pre-Christian attempts to know man and God was a paganism by virtue of its incomplete and unformed knowledge of God. This incompleteness was but a trait of the widespread desire for divine knowledge which permeated the whole Roman Empire. The hegemony of the Roman Empire was formed by the intellectual pursuits of the ancients, which culminated in the higher speculations of the Greek philosophers. The ancient Greeks had prepared man to behold the "unknown" God. The pagan religious frenzy of the mystery cults expressed man's search for God. The Roman Empire gathered men together in the civilized pursuit of God. Such is the Byzantine view of the world that met Christ: a world in which the Greek search for philosophical and divine truth had contributed to the civilized growth of man, and a realm where the hegemony afforded by the Roman Empire had made this "Greek" civilization available to the whole of the Mediterranean world. Christ was born into a Greek and Roman world that existed simply to accommodate His birth. So it is to the Byzantine that the spread of Christianity was inevitable and natural.

It is not only the Byzantine who sees the Roman Empire as a unit. The famous Belgian historian, Henri Pirenne, bases his historical view of the Roman Empire on a Mediterranean hegemony that would discount the notion of any part of the Empire being obscure, separated, and insignificant. But he sees this as a mundane hegemony, not as a divine hegemony. Even the most sophisticated Western observer, therefore, does not understand the Roman Empire from the perspective of the Byzantine. The best metaphor that the West can offer is one of the stew of civilization being spiced by the religious and cultural additives of Christianity. This is a metaphor far removed from that of the Orthodox thinker, who sees the Greek civilization of the Roman Empire as the collection of condiments and spices, formed, under divine direction, into a sometimes bitter and tasteless blend, to which were added the substance, body, and ingredients of Christianity —thereby offering man a divine food and mundane taste of the heavenly.

It was into a Roman Empire united by its common Greek culture, then, that the Byzantine pictures the advent of Jesus Christ. The Church which preserved and preached His message was Roman, by virtue of the world in which it functioned, but Greek in its spirit and its expression. The Apostles spread Christianity primarily in the Greek tongue, even in the capital city of the Empire, Rome, where Latin was a ceremonial and official language, Greek the *lingua franca*. The philosophers, who early on in the spread of Christianity formed its theological expression, did so in the categories of Greek thought. And the first written records of the Christian Church, the letters of the Apostle Paul and others, along with the Gospels of the Evangelists, were written and presented in Greek. The Christians taken to Rome, during the great persecutions, came from all parts of the Empire and represented the many nationalities and races that had converted to the Christian religion, as it spread through the medium of the Greek cultural hegemony that united these various peoples. The witness of so many Christians from so many parts of the Empire left a lasting and foreboding impression on the Roman capital.

According to the Acts of the Apostles, it was St. Paul who first taught Christianity in Rome. It is he, say the Orthodox, who is the actual founder of that Church (perhaps together with St. Peter —here the authorities differ). And this is only appropriate, since St. Peter's presence in the city would have been that of an Apostle who only slowly accepted that Christianity belonged to all nations. It was St. Paul, the "Apostle of the Nations," who so indefatigably strove to present the Christian message to the whole Roman Empire, his presence in Rome, the most cosmopolitan of cities, the gathering place of people from all the known world, signifying the universal or "catholic" character of the Christian Church. The honor of being a Christian in Rome was precisely that of representing all of Christianity, an honor which expressed the hegemony of the Empire in Christian catholicity.

The spiritual center of Christianity, however, was not Rome. This fundamental concept guides the Byzantine understanding of the Early Church. One must never confuse the catholicity of Christianity with the images which express that catholicity. This point the Orthodox Church has always stressed with particular fervor. The honor due Rome in the Early Church was a derived honor —an honor derived from the universality which the Roman capital epitomized. As for the argument that the Christian Church in Rome held an *actual* primacy in the Church, rather than one of honor —this would have struck the primitive Church as being absurd. Also, to trace that primacy to St. Peter, the "Prince" of the Apostles, would not have seemed sensible. If, indeed, some personal primacy, aside from that of Christ, had existed in the Church, would it not have belonged to St. James, the first Bishop of Jerusalem and kinsman of the Lord, who according to the Acts of the Apostles presided over the first Council of the Apostles (that in which the issue of the catholicity of the Christian message was decided —a decision betrayed by St. Peter's later actions in Antioch)? And the Virgin Mary having been alive at the same time that there was a Bishop in Rome, need one ask which would have had primacy in the Church, had such a notion of primacy existed? Christ built His Church, the Orthodox assert, on St. Peter's confession of Christ's divinity: "Thou art the Christ, the Son of the living God." That confession is the rock, the cornerstone, upon which the Church stands. (See St. Matthew 16: 16-18). Neither St. Paul, the actual founder of the Church of Rome, nor St. Peter, perhaps the co-founder of that Church, ever held any *actual* primacy in the Church. Nor did any city. Such notions are ludicrous to the Eastern Christian, for Christian primacy rests squarely upon the divinity of Christ.

The institutional, or symbolic role of the capital of the Empire in the development of Christianity continued, however, to grow. But here again, Rome was not the focus of this growth. It was in the New Rome, in the city of Constantinople —where St. Constantine the Emperor had moved the seat of the Empire at the beginning of the fourth century—, that the symbolic center of Christianity was established. The same honor that had been given to Old Rome by the persecuted Christians was given also to New Rome, with the coming of the official recognition of Christianity by the Roman Emperor. Old Rome had joined Constantinople, New Rome, the former city of Byzantium, and the primacy of honor came to be shared by these two great capitals. The fact of this sharing —a fact acknowledged by the undivided Christian Church in the Second Oecumenical Synod in 381)— alone dispels any notion of there having been a single center of ecclesiastical authority in the ancient Church. It was a primacy of honor that was shared, not a rivalry for primacy as such.

For the Byzantine, the Empire, as the structure into which the Church was integrated, was not a power that, because of increasing strength and numbers in Christianity, had capitulated to this new force. It existed for the very purpose of accommodating the

Christian Church. Thus the Emperor Constantine was genuinely enlightened from within to favor the Christian religion, having been convinced of its power by a miraculous image of the Holy Cross that promised him victory in battle. His participation in the theological debates and dialogues that helped safeguard and standardize the Christian beliefs and traditions which had reached his age from the time of the Apostles was, therefore, not —as prevailing historical theories would have it— an attempt to sway the Christian Church towards a theology of his liking. His participation grew out of his internal knowledge and acceptance of the divinely ordained role of the Roman Empire in the spread of Christianity. It is not a great life of piety or a martyric confession of Christianity that ultimately makes the Emperor Constantine what he is. His simple acknowledgement of his role and the role of his Empire in the Christian scheme made him a Saint, an Equal-to-the-Apostles —the human through whom the divine mission of Christianity was made manifest. Such is the sublime Byzantine answer to the mundane historical portrait of St. Constantine offered by the Western or Latin-minded Orthodox historian.

When the Germanic barbarians invaded the Western part of the Roman Empire, reaching finally the Eternal City, Old Rome, the smaller Western part of the Empire was cut off from the wealthy power center of New Rome, Constantinople. Though the Roman Empire continued to grow and prosper in the East, it entered a period of decline in the West, the Western Church concentrating its organization in Old Rome, in an attempt to fill the power gap left by the withering political and secular leadership. Cut off from the vast majority of the Church, which flourished in the Eastern provinces of the Roman Empire and around the new capital in Constantinople, the Roman Bishop took on greater and greater responsibility for the spread of Christianity in the Western segments of the Empire. What little of civilization that would survive in the West would survive under his direction. But never, the Byzantines have always asserted, did the Pope interpret his role as anything but one demanded by the exigencies of the times. In fact, Pope Gregory I (the Great) (d. 604), misunderstanding the authority assumed by the Bishop of New Rome, wrote some rather terse words to the Patriarch in Constantinople, warning that he should not misinterpret or overstate the primacy of honor due him as the Bishop of New Rome. St. Gregory clearly points out that actual *authority* in the Church is shared by all Bishops equally. Indeed, he obviously had a clear understanding of the uncommon circumstances under which the Bishop of Rome, after the fall of the West, came to hold certain extraordinary secular and ecclesiastical powers. Neither did he abuse these circumstances, nor did he wish the Bishop of New Rome to be tempted by any abuse of *his* status of honor. His —and this from a Pope of Rome— is the clearest witness against a primacy of authority in the Roman Pontiff.

The decline of the West took a great toll on the Empire, and the rise of the Franks (Germanic tribes) to power in the Western provinces estranged those provinces from the bulk of the Roman Empire. The power and riches of Rome were denied the citizens of Old Rome, and their culture soon came to naught. When, in the ninth century, the Franks themselves began to experience cultural growth, the Byzantines looked upon this phenomenon with interest. But by no means did they understand this growth as a rebirth of the Roman Empire. Their only understanding of the Carolingian Renaissance was its interaction with the Church, the only legitimate arm of the Roman Empire that it considered to have survived in the West. And this understanding was soon to be colored by confusion and strife; for, indeed, in its years of estrangement from the Empire, the See of Old Rome had developed some rather curious notions.

Among those things which the Byzantines found curious in the so-called "Holy Roman Empire" — which they saw as neither holy nor Roman, but quite secular and Germanic— was an increasing tendency on the part of the Roman Pontiff to assume exactly the magnitude and scope of power against which St. Gregory the Great had so sternly warned the Patriarch of Constantinople. (We might incidentally note here that the words "Pope" and "Patriarch" were used commonly in the Early Church to refer to Bishops of important historical Sees. "Pope" is not a designation reserved only for the Bishop of Rome, as many today erroneously think.) The misgivings of the Byzantines can best be illustrated by their astonishment at a document which most scholars believe had its origins in the late eighth or ninth century: the Donation of Constantine. It purports to be a document in which the Emperor Constantine bequeathed his secular power to the Pope of Rome. This document, actually a forgery, represents the kind of claim to power that surfaced in Rome during the ninth century. It was in fact put forth in a serious argument for the primacy of the Bishop of Rome, both in the Church and the Empire, by Pope Leo IX (b. 1002), one of the Frankish Pontiffs, in his dispute with the Byzantines. The Byzantines were bemused, if perplexed, at the thought that Leo could have seriously considered the Germanic Empire the successor to the Empire of Rome, let alone the idea that the Bishop of Rome was the supreme ruler of the Church and this would-be Empire. That these claims were further made on the basis of a clumsy attempt at legitimacy based on a document forged by half-literate barbarians was something that simply astonished the sophisticated Byzantines.

More importantly, the Byzantines faced a theological challenge from the Carolingian theologians. They could hardly take seriously the emperorship of Charlemagne, a potentate who could probably do little more than sign his name —if that! His claims constituted an incredible effrontery. But the theological innovations of the Franks they took quite seriously. They were quite concerned, in their encounters with the Frankish theologians, about the divergent course of theological thinking in the new Germanic realm. They were further disturbed by the fact that this thinking was characterized by the Franks as a continuation of the Latin theological tradition. The Byzantines knew a Latin theological tradition that had been nurtured and formed in the Greek hegemony of the primitive Church. That tradition was consistent with the Greek Patristic witness, though, especially after St. Augustine of Hippo (b. 354), perhaps potentially innovative. But what the Franks were offering was wholly out of keeping with the consensus of the Church, in the minds of the Byzantines.

Unlike the Westerner, the Eastern Christian sees the first schism in the Church in the departure of the non-Chalcedonian Eastern Churches from Orthodox belief in the fifth century. The great Christological debates that had led so many believers in the Levant to split from Orthodox thought, therefore, were fresh in the minds of the Byzantines. They were acutely aware of the Orthodox consensus which had emerged from the Church Councils that met to safeguard the ancient Christian beliefs handed down from Apostolic times. With this awareness came a great wariness, on the part of the Byzantines, at the distortion of the Nicene-Constantinopolitan Creed (the Creed endorsed by the whole Church, East and West) by the Frankish theologians. In the formula describing the "procession" of the Holy Spirit, the words "and the Son" (the so-called *filioque* clause) had been inserted, as an expression of theological clarity, by the Carolingians. Until relatively lately, modern historians, insensitive as they are to the outlook of the Byzantines, believe that the Eastern response to this insertion is nothing less than inane. They point out that the theological views of the Franks, while perhaps petty from a modern standpoint, actually have their roots in certain Byzantine theological thinkers. They see the Eastern Church's response to this issue as "fatuous" and "imbecilic," to use some of the more common expressions of Western polemicists.

In actual fact, it is the Western observer who is imbecilic in his evaluation, if he fails to realize that it was the Byzantine appeal to the *consensus* of Orthodox opinion, the very foundation of the Church of the Empire, which was at issue in the filioque dispute. They were not concerned with minority views that might have linked the Carolingians with earlier Christian thought. The wariness of the Byzantines stemmed directly from their perception of a threat against this consensus, a consensus, as we have noted, that they had seen shattered by the refusal of some Eastern Churches to accept the formulations of the Council of Chalcedon (451) regarding the nature of Christ. For them, any departure from the agreed-upon confessions of the Church was a departure from the catholicity of the Church. They were quite naturally apprehensive, moreover, about a dispute which hinged on Christological arguments, as did any theological debate over the nature of the Trinity. For them, the arrogance of the Frankish theologians, in departing from the consensual theology of the Church, was secondary to the danger of the Church of Rome establishing itself as an authority separate from the witness of the whole Church. And, given the emergence of Papal claims to rather extensive power, the Byzantines were not excessive in their concerns. They had every reason to believe that, isolated from the Empire, a new (and unnecessary) role thrust upon him by the power vacuum created with the collapse of the political arm of the Western sector of the Empire, the Bishop of Rome had led his followers on a course divergent from that of the vast majority of the Empire. And they had no reason to believe that the theological divergences of the Carolingian theologians were anything but the consequences of that course.

The parting of ways of the Byzantine, the Roman Empire, and the Franks in the ninth century set in motion a process of estrangement that finally ended in the eleventh century with the mutual excommunication of the Orthodox Church and the Church of Rome. Western historians, ignoring the years of separation that preceded this schism, often wish to present the split as the result of a personality dispute betwen a Papal emissary to Constantinople and the Ecumenical Patriarch of the Eastern Church. This is an inadequate assessment of the affair. Firstly, the Ecumenical Patriarch is, in the Orthodox world, one of many Bishops, holding only a primacy of honor ("first among equals") and having no authority to take such a precipitous step as that of excommunicating, on a personal whim, a large portion of the Church. What transpired between the Patriarch and the Papal legate was simply an outcome of the fact that the Church of Rome no longer fit into the theological consensus that was the Church of the Empire. Secondly, the accounts of the actual exchange of excommunications, while not our particular concern here, have often been presented in the West in rather self-serving and hardly objective ways.

For the Byzantines, 1054 was that date at which the final separation of the Churches, long divided in their beliefs and spiritual outlook, was accomplished. The Bishop of Rome, having set a course that separated him and his followers from the traditions of the Early Church —largely preserved in the East, its beliefs, in turn, codified in Councils that, while accepted in the West, had a largely Eastern character— had fallen away from the Orthodox theological consensus. The Pope had separated himself from the Roman Empire, from the ancient Sees of the Christian Church (including the Mother Church, the first Church of Christendom, in Jerusalem and the Church where Christians had first been known by that name, that of Antioch), and from the Christian hegemony which had so long protected the Faith. He had joined the non-Chalcedonians in yet another schism, and he, like them, had partially precipitated this split by estranging himself from the general conscience of the Church. Indeed, in 1054 the Church of Rome, one —and only one— of the ancient Churches, had separated itself from the Church which had been preserved in the East since the time of the Apostles. So the Byzantines saw the "Great Schism" of 1054.

After 1054, there was little formal contact between

Eastern and Western Christians, despite lingering associations in certain outposts of the Byzantine (Roman) Empire. This lamentable separation was ended, however, in an equally lamentable period of history. In the fifteenth century, with the Byzantines beset by invasions by the Moslems, the Orthodox Church, for primarily political reasons, turned to the West for aid in protecting the Empire which had so long protected the Church. Given the fact that the Orthodox clergy went to Rome for political reasons, hoping to find aid from the West in saving the threatened Empire, it is not strange that the attempts at ecclesiastical union were unsuccessful. In fact, the Orthodox to this day recount the period as one in which the West required humiliating concessions from the Orthodox, extracting some agreements by actual force. Moreover, the fact that a Roman Crusade had, in 1204, sacked the Christian capital of Constantinople, pillaging, destroying holy places, and plundering Churches and monasteries, gave the Byzantine diplomats the impression that they were dealing with enemies to begin with, not allies. At any rate, when the Roman Empire fell to Mohammed II in 1453, the Byzantines were heard to murmur their preference for the Turkish turban over the Papal tiara. The Western world having just entered the dawn of the Renaissance, the Byzantine world entered its long age of darkness and horror under the yoke of Islam.

The Orthodox Church experienced no Reformation. The task of carrying on the Empire passed on to the Russians, whom the Orthodox had converted in the tenth century. Through modern times, that Church, however, has also suffered at the hands of enemies. The old Byzantines, those who had formed the Eastern part of the Roman Empire, remained under the rule of Islam until the mid-nineteenth century, some even well into the twentieth century. Their enemies were clear and well defined. The new Byzantines, those who belonged to the so-called Third Rome (a relatively modern and quite incorrect appellation for Moscow, based on a wholly faulty understanding of imperial Byzantium), had enemies of a decidedly more subtle kind. The Russians were constantly bombarded by Western thought, Western theologies, and at times by Western armies. In fact, many Orthodox in Western Europe were converted by the sword to Roman Catholicism —those who had not succumbed to the double-edged sword of fascination with the Western world, which brought with it both cultural development and world-views incompatible with the tenets of the Orthodox Faith. Keeping their external Orthodox customs, but having the heart of the Orthodox Faith cut away, many Eastern European Greek Catholics have survived to this day, the spoils of the Western invasion of the East. The history of Russia is the history of the new Byzantines, trying with all of their souls to remain Eastern, to hold to the ancient consensus of the Roman Empire. And when their history succeeded at this, it was a glorious history, that of a truly Holy Russia, fragrant with Christian antiquity; when their history failed them, the Russians were a sad and tragic people. Their Orthodox beliefs became artificial, Westernized, distorted, and fanciful.

This is Orthodoxy as it came into the twentieth century. It was, in the case of the Russians, just emerging from a Western captivity in many circles of society and, to a large extent, in its theology (though this captivity is often overstated, at the expense of counter-trends that mark the period of Russian history immediately prior to the Revolution). The old Byzantines, the inheritors of the ancient Roman

world, were just shaking off the shackles of an en-
slavement which only poets like Byron really cared
to understand, and which Westerners have, oddly
enough, tended to characterize as "charitable." Aside
from the fact that slavery can never be charitable, the
numberless victims of violence, horrendous torture,
and barbarism (which Westerners can perhaps better
understand in the light of recent growth in Islamic
fundamentalism) should be imprinted on the Western consciousness and historical memory. That it is
not is understandable. When the Orthodox world
emerged into the twentieth century, the West had
forgotten its own past. It had forgotten its own
"roots." It had forgotten where it got its Christian civilization. Thus, when the Russian Empire fell to the
horror of communism, few in the West really understood the ominous meaning of this event. No one
really understood that an inheritor of the glory of the
past had fallen to the ignominy of the arrogant
present.

To understand the Orthodox Church in modern
times, we might observe, demands efforts of Gargan-
tuan magnitude. One must free himself, initially,
from the truncated historiographies of the West. He
must find the true past of the Western world. Then
he must free himself from the theological supposi-
tions which have formed the popular Western theologies. Only then can he prepare himself to grasp
what the Orthodox tradition is. But here the task
only begins. The Orthodox have survived the trials
of history with their spirit intact, but they have lost
many of the privileges of self-presentation. Convert
Greek Catholics, products of a spirit which is not
wholly Orthodox, are sometimes the most affluent
and vocal representatives of Orthodoxy in the West.
Orthodox are themselves falling to the historiogra-

phies and prejudices of the West. Of late, partly because of the Patriarchate's efforts to improve its con-
ditions under the yoke of Turkish persecution in
Constantinople, and partly because the large number
of former Greek Catholics who have come into the
Church are less uncomfortable with such compromise and betrayal and thus support it with their
money and influence, a theory of papism has begun
to emerge in the Oecumenical Patriarchate. Forget-
ting the foundations of Orthodox ecclesiology, some
Westernized Orthodox have fallen to the error of be-
lieving that canonical Orthodoxy is tied to communion with Constantinople, and thus that the pro-
unionist stand of that Patriarchate vis-à-vis Rome
somehow has catholic sanction within the Orthodox
Church. To know the real Orthodox world, then, one
can scarcely depend on the witness of modern times.
We must reach back into history, searching for an authenticity that is hidden under centuries and layers
of misunderstanding and self-serving historical am-
nesia. Reaching back in this way, we find a unique,
singular witness, calling itself the criterion of truth
itself. This criterion is seldom sought or appreciated
by the modern historical and religious world, Orthodox or not. To do so, however, is to be an honest
man. To find the true Byzantine heritage, we might
say, is to join in a consensus that stretches across the
expanse of Western civilization. As elusive as it is
true, this consensus brings us, Easterner and Westerner alike, closer to what we truly are —closer to
our true identities.

Chapter II

THEOLOGY IN THE EAST AND WEST

A Contrast

Within the scope of a short essay, it is impossible to summarize the differences between Eastern Orthodox and Roman Catholic theology. We have no intention of even pretending to approach such a goal. What we would like to do, in discussing the divergent Eastern and Western views of theology, is to pursue the course followed in the foregoing overview of the Byzantine and Western notions of Christian ecclesiastical history. Just as people have a basic notion of where their religions come from, so they have a general outline or schema of their beliefs. It is this informal, perhaps intuitive idea that Easterners and Westerners have about Christian belief that we would like to capture. This contrast of ideas will not, of course, constitute a technical exposition of either Roman Catholic or Eastern Orthodox belief. The common ideas that all of us hold about God, man, the Church, and so on are seldom if ever cogent, articulate statements that perfectly reflect the Christian truth. Especially for the Eastern Orthodox Christian, theological thinking is something which only approximates the truth. Indeed, in the Byzantine scheme of things, even when a thinker's writings are considered divinely inspired, it rarely earns him the title "theologian." (Only several theological thinkers, because of their lofty writings on the nature of God, have been called "theologians" in the Orthodox

Church —indeed officially only three.) This is probably rightly so, since if, as we Christians believe, our religion relates to the "Truth of truths," then its ultimate expression is ontological and noumenal, existing beyond the world of mere description and "theologizing," as we normally understand the latter term. Let us not think that what we intend here, then, is something dogmatic or a *theological summa*.

We will begin our discussion of theology where it should begin: with God. The Western world is essentially concerned with the question of whether or not God exists. This is not an overstatement, since the medieval Western theologians, in their various attempts at philosophical "proofs" of the existence of God, bequeathed to modern secular philosophy a concern for this issue that can be seen in thinkers so diverse as Descartes, Kant, or Bertrand Russell. It would be safe to say that a very significant part of Western philosophical thought is dedicated to the question of God's existence, whether directly or peripherally. So it is that even today it is not unusual for an intellectual to classify himself as a "believer," an "atheist," or, in the case of the less bold, an "agnostic." The question of the existence of God lies at the very foundation of our intellectual self-knowledge, like it or not. The way that a Westerner discusses religion, the religious experience, and most aspects of theology is tied in a fundamental way to the question of God's existence.

To a large extent, we believe in God in the West because we have "faith"; that is, we use this informal definition of a complex theological term to characterize the intellectual "leap of faith" by which we affirm that God exists. This leap itself can be based on certain observations about the world (who set all of the laws of the universe into motion?), leading at times to a form of Deism; or, it can proceed forth from personal " revelatory intuition" based on an inner understanding that God exists, an informal, personal feeling about the existence of a Creator —a kind of emotional *a priori*, as it were. This is why many Western religious thinkers derive God from observations about nature (this is as old as St. Augustine in Western thought and even has some roots in the Eastern Fathers of the primitive Church), while others look to an "inner God." On the whole, however sophisticated his theological notions about God, the common Westerner usually begins with this first "leap of faith," this first act of establishing belief. Indeed, his basic encounters with the religious are encounters essentially shaped by a basic faith in the fact that God exists.

Once it is established that God exists, either by deriving the notion of a prime mover from observations about nature or by turning inward to the impulses of the self, most Westerners begin to anthropomorphize God. This is a greatly bold statement and one which almost every Westerner would find presumptuous, if not downright outrageous. Nonetheless, in those honest moments when "faith" in God's existence comes under fire, almost every Westerner will admit to thinking of God as the "Great Clockmaker" or the "gentle God within." And more often than not, both visions of God reduce to a childish image of an old man with a grey beard. This is only logical. A notion of God that focuses on His existence is bound to be anthropomorphic. Whether we see God in nature or in ourselves, we quite naturally seek Him out in a very human way: in the form of nature and its most intricate product (man), or directly in the form of man himself. It is disconcerting, no doubt, for the sophisticated Westerner to read

such words. Certainly not *everyone in* the West —we
would object— thinks in such a way about God. But
this perturbation probably comes to us because we
know that all too many Westerners do, in fact, think
of God exactly in this way. A God who takes form in
our efforts to prove His existence, we might argue,
will certainly have the "empirical" traits that our
methods of inquiry dictate. If we look at our environ-
ment, God will have an observable form. If we look
within ourselves, God will undoubtedly have a very
personal, human form (which perhaps makes
Freud's concept of God as an internalized "father figure" so compelling to the atheistic or agnostic Westerner).

We might further establish this argument about
the Western concept of God by approaching the matter from the standpoint of the non-existence of God.
What is it that a Western atheist rejects, when he
says that he does not believe in God. Inevitably, he
rejects an anthropomorphic understanding of God.
The end-product of classical analysis, for example, is
one's supposed freedom from the autocratic domi-
nance of the internalized authority figure —from the
autocratic "father image" which haunts the psyche.
The modern scientist, rejecting the anthropomorphic
vision of a divine clockmaker, moves from such a
vividly human image to one of a disembodied
"force" or some amorphous "divine catalyst." In effect, the Western atheist simply casts off an anthropomorphic view of God. He casts off a mental image.
(There are, however, the so-called atheists of the
scientific world who have dressed God, their "old
man with the grey beard," in the robes of "Mother
Nature." But these closet Deists are quite secretive!)
Indeed, the very pursuit of "proofs" for the existence
of God has led most Westerners into the trap of an-

thropomorphism —staking their religious outlook on the acceptance or rejection of a deity derived from observation or from the self.

Let us not deny, of course, that there are Westerners who, in all of this, rise above an anthropomorphic view of God and who neither accept nor reject the idea of God on the basis of empirical or philosophical "proofs" of His existence. Moreover, if we posit that God does indeed exist, there is no reason to believe that His reality (or nature, for that matter) is in any way compromised by the limitations of human thought about Him. This is certainly not the substance of our argument here. What we are saying is that the Western view of God is so basically tied to the notion of evidence about His existence, that this inevitability clouds a Westerner's vision, even when he does confront and experience the reality of God. This is especially evident, as we have noted, in the case of the Western atheist. He is so committed to his rejection of a limited view of God —the very notion of rejection being dictated by the Western preoccupation with the question of God's existence— that he is not inclined to think about the obvious issue of the inadequacy of his limited view of God. Beginning with the proposition that God's existence is the starting place of religion, the West has created, tragically enough, a pre-defined God Who either exists or does not exist.

The Byzantine begins with quite a different idea of God. The question for him is not whether or not God exists, but how man can understand and reach God. At first, this approach does not seem so unique to the Westerner. But this is because he does not take it seriously enough. Quite literally, the Byzantines begin theologizing with an *assumption* that God exists. This is not an assumption derived from nature, nor is it merely an intuitive assumption. It is something more than that. It is an assumption made on a noumenal, ontological plane. It corresponds to the assumption which introduces the Gospel of St. John the Evangelist, "In the beginning was the Word...," and which was known to the ancient Jews: "In the beginning God created...." One does not, in Byzantine theology, look within to establish the existence of God. Nor does he look to things external to him, to things in the created world. Rather, he begins the spiritual ascent with "faith," with a "spiritual fact," a firm unquestioned part of his cognitive world. This is revelation in a higher way, in a way that is independent of human intuition and reasoning, which is part of the human condition, implicit in being human —to be taken as simply and as concretely as the creation statement in Genesis: "God created."

For the Byzantines, the question of God's existence was essentially a superficial one. God is what is and what is not; that is, He encompasses all that we are and know and all that we are not and cannot know. He is known to us in His energies, as St. Gregory Palamas (b. 1296), the great teacher of hesychasm, asserts, but He also abides in His essence. Through His energies, we can know God, both as He is made manifest in the world and within us; in His essence, however, He can never be known, since His essence cannot be circumscribed by human thought. Essentially, as a consequence of this concept of God, a Byzantine thinker cannot be an atheist. The God Whom he rejects as not existing would be encompassed by the unknowable essence of God —by that part of God that transcends existence. The God Whom he would reject because of His anthropomorphic qualities would likewise exist, since His energies (the only source of such an anthropomorphic vision of God) would be encompassed by His essence, which is by definition not anthropomorphic. In actuality, however, the question of atheism has not traditionally been a burning one in the Christian East, since the very notion of God is not approached from the standpoint of his existence or non-existence.

All of this does not mean that the Eastern Christian does not, at times, have an anthropomorphic vision of God. Not at all. There exist among Easterners, as among Westerners, those simple folk who envision God as an old man with a long beard. But this belief is not, for the Easterner, the consequence of a "theology" which begins with a need for establishing God's existence. It is the simple consequence of the frailty of the human mind and its inability to capture God. And everywhere in the Byzantine religious world this frailty is presented as just that: a frailty. Therefore, if one questions the existence of his anthropomorphic God, he actually questions himself about his human limitations in understanding and grasping the true nature of God. Since these anthropomorphic limitations rise out of man's own inadequacies, he never attributes them to God; for, unlike the Westerner, his God does not rise out of these limitations. His God is not derived from the world or from the self. His struggle is not with God's existence, but with the limitations that his own existence places on him in understanding God. His search for God is of a different kind than that of the Westerner. And ultimately, it must be admitted, his experience of God is different.

There is a great divergence, too, in the way that Eastern Orthodox and Roman Catholics see man and his relationship to God —that is, in the very way that they understand salvation and even Christ. Beginning probably with St. Augustine, the West developed a view of man that is not wholly consistent with that presented in the primitive Church and preserved in the contemporary Orthodox theology. It was Augustine's understanding —and one can see this so clearly in his *Confessions*— that man has somehow violated the law of God, that he is in need of compensating for this violation, and that his own self-dissatisfaction (which he feels when he observes the evil of the world around him) prompts him to avail himself of the salvific Sacrifice of Christ. The expiation afforded by the death of Christ, St. Augustine argued, was proper atonement for the sin of Adam and Eve, removing from the human the innate effects of original sin. While the writings of this renowned Church Father themselves are only *flawed* by certain deviations from the consensus thinking of the Early Church (and are replete, one must note, with awesome and magnificent insights into the very core of Christian Truth), those who followed him, amplifying these deviations, transformed his outlook into a rigid, legalistic one. And this legalism was inherited by Roman Catholicism (and to an extent by the Protestant West).

The common idea that has developed in the West since the time of St. Augustine is that man, if he looks at his world, perceives that things are not as they should be. If he ponders the presence of evil, disease, and death in the world, he will realize that some literal curse hangs over mankind. If he further accepts the revealed theology of the Church, he will understand that man, having inherited from Adam and Eve a sentence of death for transgressing the law of the Creator, is born into the world condemned under the law, bearing this condemnation as original sin. Christ, God incarnate, satisfied the law by taking upon Himself the sin of man, thus showing both the ineffable mercy of God and opening up to man the possibility of overcoming original sin. By participating in the Sacrifice of Christ, by seeking atonement through His death, the human can hope to be rewarded with a return to immortality, to a life free from evil, disease, and death, in the afterlife. By failing to participate in the Sacrifice of Christ, by indulging his original sin and his inclination towards evil, the human being is punished by God, suffering his just rewards for the innate sin of all mankind.

What the foregoing juridical theories often produce in the practical religious life of the West is the thought that if one is good, if he does those things which Christ did, he will be rewarded with Heaven. If, on the other hand, he does those things which are natural to man, he will be punished with Hell. The West has even developed a theology of good works, in which the successful imitation of Christ, realized through acts of charity and unselfish service, is thought to "merit" an individual his salvation. The Protestant reformers were especially opposed to this theology and reacted by putting forth a formula that predicated man's salvation on faith alone. But in effect both Roman Catholics *and* Protestants operate from a reward and punishment model, it making little difference whether one posits that the reward can be earned by works or that it proceeds from faith alone. There are, of course, refinements of how each Roman Catholic theologian or Protestant tradition conceptualizes both the theoretical and practical aspects of this view of man. We have presented a decidedly simplistic portrayal of a complex view. Yet, even with these reservations in mind, what we have said constitutes a valid portrayal. This any objective observer will admit.

We might note here, perhaps incidentally, that

the juridical or legalistic concept of man and salvation proffered in the West is not without its tragic
elements. It is so juridical —such an overstatement
of a single Patristic model— that it seems threaten-
ing. When reduced to matters of practical applica-
tion, moreover, it is often devastating. In a very legalistic way, this concept avers that man is born into
the world as a sinful creature, having inherited from
some distant ancestors the sentence of death. When
detached from the context of the moving soul-
searching of spiritual seekers like St. Augustine,
when overstated, and when made cold, this idea
makes God appear almost "unjust." Furthermore,
the human being becomes hopelessly beset by sin, all
that is natural to him —all that rises out of his human impulses— appearing sinful. God is transformed into a very distant judge who, as a reward for
our good works (or for our Faith, as the Reformers
insist), will give us rest from our sin in the afterlife
or, if we fail in the task of overcoming our very na-
tures, will punish us with eternal torment. While
this vision, if taken as a faulty description of the actual state of things, can make us sober, it can, because of
its juridical presentation in Western religious
thought, also provoke disbelief or opposition to God.
Many Western thinkers, assessing this concept of
man and salvation and seeing it as a mere legal con-
tract, reject it as faulty. Its tone is so cold and so ratio-
nalistic that it never touches on the internal human
intuitions about man that it is supposed to express. It
breeds, all too often, a disdain for the religious.

The Eastern Orthodox view of man and salvation
is in no sense juridical. It does not present to man an
overstated scheme, but rather proceeds from the human being's understanding of himself, his world,
and his history. In the first place, in the Christian

East one does not understand man to be a fallen creature because of *personal* observations about humandkind and the world. The East received from the ancient philosophers and from the saga of the Jews an understanding of history of that conveys to man a certain memory of his lost past. History, after all, should tell us where we are. And that is just what history tells the Eastern Christian: it preserves in him a nostalgia for the higher aspects of man and for those divine qualities which he has lost. As well, history and philosophy serve to awaken in man a sense of his higher potential, of his participation in the divine economy. Original sin, or the "ancestral sin," is nothing more or less than man's separation from his true and original nature, a "curse" passed down from his spiritual ancestors. It is intimately tied to his very awareness that he is somehow not what he should be. It is his tragic sense of having lost a path set out for him by God, but from which he has deviated. Original sin, rather than defining the innately sinful nature of the human, serves to bring him to an awareness of his innate divinity, of his higher side. It serves to contrast what he is, in his fallen state, with what he should and can be.

Orthodox theology does not emphasize the expiatory nature of Christ's Sacrifice over and above the consequences of that Sacrifice, the restoration of Adam and Eve to their former state of purity. Christ's redemptive act is, for the Orthodox Christian, a merciful act of condescension by which God has redeemed the human from his transgression against the course which God freely offered him (the most important expression of man's free will and one which did not engender the curious arguments about that subject which for so long beset Western theology). By Christ's Sacrifice, man is offered anew the opportunity to pursue a divine course. His distorted world, through the Resurrection of Christ, has been put into proper order. God, having become man, broke the curse of death which man had imposed, by his deviant course, upon himself. In the words of the ancient Fathers, Christ became man, so that man might become divine —so that he might embrace, express, and realize the divinity of a created being who participates in the divine nature of God, His Creator.

Heaven for the Eastern Christian is the final attainment of man's proper nature, of his divinity within God. (The Orthodox Fathers stress that man participates in the energies of God, though never in His essence. In this way, of course, the created being who is man never usurps the unknowable majesty of God Himself, Who is beyond man's comprehension.) But because original sin is a curse, a stain, and because man can cultivate his divine nature through the Sacrifice of Christ, the path towards Heaven begins on earth. The spiritual life is not one only of imitating Christ, but of participating in the divine nature, of uniting oneself to Christ —of undergoing θέωσις, or divinization— here on earth. In this process, man reaches to the highest state of perfection, such that, though his sinful nature is present to him, he acts, rather, from his inclinations towards the holy. Life on earth, if it cultivates the divine nature of man, clouds and muffles the passionate impulses of sin, making the human on earth partly divine. A person restored to divine form (to the extent that this is possible in a corrupted body), calls all around him to holiness and divinity. He inspires in those who can see with spiritual eyes a similar spiritual quest. He combats the negative forces of the fallen world (the demons and Satan). His role on earth is that of a warrior against evil, being armed by his partial presence in Heaven itself. At his death, his battle ended, he is granted the fruits of his efforts in the spiritual world, these to be fully revealed and bestowed at the General Judgment, when all mankind will be called to account for its spiritual state.

A man who approaches Heaven while still on earth, who undergoes divinization, who gives birth to Christ, is known, to the Orthodox, as a Saint. So much does he elevate the flesh that at times (aswitnessed by the countless instances of this in the history of the Orthodox Church —right up to the present) his body does not decay at death. Indeed, his very physical substance is touched and permeated by the divine —transformed by an encounter with the energies of its Creator. These men and women, being united to Christ, having become "sons of God within the Son of God," as one Father puts it, are examples of the spiritual life to which every human is called. These Saints are veritable manifestations of Christ and are therefore venerated and honored as such. By the same token, the Virgin Mary, the *Theotokos* or "Bearer of God," who took the divine into her own body, is venerated and honored as an image of the divinity to which mankind is called. She represents, in the image of St. Maximos the Confessor, every man's potential for giving birth to Christ —she in a *bodily* way, we *spiritually*—, for uniting himself to Christ.

Hell for the Orthodox believer is not merely a place where punishment handed down by God is put into effect. Hell is a consequence of man's intransigence, the result of his inability to overcome the fallen human proclivity for sin and his failure to cultivate the divine nature of man revealed in the example and expiatory Sacrifice of Christ. Hell is a separation from man's proper nature, a perverted place of torment to which man is led by evil disobedience and through the works of its personification, Satan. It is a place of torment and torture not because God so wills it, however, but because man so deems it. It is not a place from which God has withheld His love —indeed, some Fathers teach that the greatest abundance of God's love and compassion is present to those in the fires of Gehenna—, but a place where man's rejection of that love prevails. A creature formed in the divine image, free to distort and stain that image, bound ultimately to that distortion by a willful rejection of his divine impulses, tenaciously holding to a world-view which compromises his true calling —can such a creature suffer anything but torment and unthinkable anguish at the loss of the majesty for which he was formed?

The perceptive reader will, in confronting the Orthodox view of man and salvation, sense something very special about this view. It is not a juridical metaphor. It does not pretend to be some consistent theoretical understanding of the cosmos and man. It does not begin with personal observation and move on to theological speculation. It is somehow a self-evident description of how things are, not how they might, could, or should be. This is quite simply because the Orthodox view on these matters is not "revealed" in the Western sense of "revealed theology"; it is not a derived statement about man and salvation. It is a natural statement —a true revelation— of things as they are, proceeding out of the human psyche, out of man's history, and out of the *natural* course of human thought, both theological and philosophical. One can see, by contrast to the Orthodox understanding of Saints, the Virgin Mary, or Heaven and Hell, that Western Christian notions of these things, be they Roman Catholic of Protestant, have a certain rational consistency to them that comes at the price of coldness and dryness. The Orthodox notions seem, on the other hand, intuitively true. They are too natural to be contrived. This is the uncanny way that Truth is ultimately revealed to the Orthodox Christian.

Finally, the Eastern and Western Christian worlds most significantly part ways in their understanding of the Church. Both Orthodox and Roman Catholics believe, in accordance with Scripture and history, that Christ established a Church on earth and that this Church is mystically His very Body. But for Roman Catholics, the focus of attention in understanding the Church has always been on the problem of authority (*auctoritas*). Perhaps because the Carolingians found themselves separated from the majority of the ancient centers of the Church after the collapse of the Western segment of the Roman Empire, they set the tone of the Western search for authority in their attempts to legitimize their independent course. They had, after all —as the Byzantines view matters—, separated themselves from the consensus of the Church. So, it was incumbent on them to justify their separate course. Over the years, this has been done by viewing the Church as a spiritual institution which dispenses the Grace by which salvation is attained, the authority of this institution resting in its tradition, its historical and conciliar structure, and the Papacy —the latter a legacy of the Carolingian spirit.

As regards the Church as a dispenser of the Grace by which man comes to salvation, this notion degenerated in the West, at times, into a kind of spiritual pharmaceutics. From the Early Church, the Christian religion has inherited certain metaphors about the meaning of worship, confession, ordination, marriage, and even the Eucharist itself. Worship is often spoken of in the way one speaks of mundane obligations. The personal experiences of confession and repentance have sometimes been compared to formal acts of apology and juridical practices like clemency and restitution. Ordination and marriage are often characterized as a kind of mutual bondage or servitude. And the Eucharist has been called a Divine Medicine or the Medicine of Immortality. But these metaphors have always been just that —metaphors. They are not meant to encompass the sublime Christian view of these elements of life and the way that the Church involves itself in them. Roman Catholicism has reified these metaphors. The Church, to the Westerner, is more often than not the place where Grace and salvation are almost mechanically dispensed. Worship is an obligation that includes a formal confession of sins and participation in certain ceremonies, the end result of which is an automatic attainment of justification (or salvation), The Priest becomes a functionary who, endowed with certain powers, performs the ceremonies by which this justification is effected. The fact of this legalistic approach to the Church cannot be disputed. It is the Roman Catholic Church itself which is today engaged in frantic efforts to change this common idea of the Church.

The legalistic structure of the Church —a structure to which traditional Roman Catholics have held so tenaciously— derives its authority, as we have noted, from tradition, from its historical conciliar structure, and from the Papacy. Its tradition traces to the establishment of the Roman Church on the "rock" of St. Peter. Its conciliar theology acknowledges that most Christian doctrines were formed in general Councils of the Church and that they have binding authority on the Christian, at least when the decisions of these Councils have not been disputed by Papal authority. The Papacy itself, despite the fact that the Carolingians initiated Papal claims to tremendous worldly power in the ninth century, actually never dogmatized these claims in the form of Papal infallibility until the nineteenth century. Again, one might assert that the course of the Latin Church is one largely directed by a search for authority, an authority which in its final form, as we shall see, is difficult to justify.

The authority of the Roman Church certainly does not derive from its historical primacy. As a Roman Catholic Prelate of the Greek Rite has noted, the historical liturgies of the Church (including those of ancient Rome), monasticism, and indeed the Great Synods of the Church are essentially Eastern. The traditions of the Orthodox Church are, in fact, older than those of the Church of Rome. Moreover, the Eastern Christian Churches have never believed that Christ established His Church on the "rock of St. Peter," but on the "rock" of St. Peter's confession of Christ's divinity. The Early Church had no notion like that of the modern Papacy. As for the Synods of the Church before the Great Schism which separated the Latin Church from the Orthodox East, the Pope of Rome was absent from most of them. Nor did the Synods imagine that the legitimacy of their decisions was to be determined by Papal review and approval. There are simply no historical data to support such an idea. In the end, the authority of the Roman Church rests on the one element of authority that the Carolingians tried to invoke: the Papacy. Just as the Pope is the focus of historical considerations of the Roman Church, so authority is equated with the Pope. It is no surprise, then, that a modern Pope would say, "I am tradition." Within him is contained the historical course and the power of the Church. Today the Roman Church is involved in a frenzied effort to explain its Papal claims in the face of a growing awareness, both among the Faithful and the clergy, that such claims are of dubious origins and difficult to defend by historical data.

There is no question that the Protestant Reformation was provoked by a disenchantment with the legalistic view of the Church that had developed in the pre-Reformation West. It avowedly grew out of a rejection of Papal claims to primacy, and this before such primacy had been codified in the dogma of Papal infallibility. Realizing that Papal authority was only tenuously established by Church history, the Reformers unfortunately pursued a rather singular course. Rather than consider the issue of authority in a broader historical way and in a more mystical and less functional way —and thus overlooking the Eastern witness to a large extent—, they deposed the Pope and placed the Bible in his place. They had now, not the "Sole Apostle," but *sola Scriptura*. Failing to understand that the Bible grew out of the Church (its very structure was canonized by several Synods), they seized upon it as the exclusive foundation of their faith. Having separated the Bible from the Church in which it originated and which it expresses, and having rejected the Roman Church, they lost an enduring idea of the Church itself and separated into numberless denominations. The end result, in modern times, is an ecclesiology that fundamentally denies Christ's establishment of a singular Church on earth and His promise that nothing would prevail against that Church.

The Orthodox concept of the Church is really quite simple and compelling. The Orthodox have always believed that Christ established a Church on earth. That Church is, as St. Paul expresses it, the "pillar of Truth," deriving its authority from Christ Himself. Its authority resides first of all in Christ. Its authority also rests in its power to remain the same at all times, expressing this consistency in historical tradition. The Church, like a person, has an unchanging identity that accompanies it throughout — from its birth in Jerusalem to the end of time. Though it had an infancy, and has now reached adulthood, the Church is the same Church today that it was in the past. This consistency the Orthodox Church calls Holy Tradition, the guidance of the Holy Spirit in time and space, in history. In addition, the authority of the Church rests in its general conscience, its body (which is the mystical Body of Christ). This conscience has been expressed in the Synods of the Church. Seven of these Synods are considered authoritative —not, as some westernized Orthodox authorities have wrongly claimed, because they *represented all geographical segments of the Church* gathered in one place (the Bishops of Rome, as we have said, were seldom even present at the Synods), but because they have survived *as true expressions of the "mind of the Church,"* of her identity, indeed of her conscience.

The function of the Church is that of the Ark in the Old Testament. It is a place where sinners living in a world bent on destruction gather for spiritual nourishment and safety, passing over the flood waters of life to the harbor of salvation. Those who serve up the spiritual food by which man's soul is regenerated and nourished, the clergy, are servants taking upon themselves the responsibility of feeding the lay people. They are servants within the Royal Priesthood of the people of God. And the Bishops who guide the Ark of Salvation are not the ultimate authority of the Church; they are guides who, as images or "icons" of Christ, by the very direction of Christ move the Ark to its destination. The Church is therefore a "home," a haven, a world within the world for the Orthodox Christian, and its function is natural and organic. Authority (ἐξουσία) rests in every aspect of its movement toward the divine. There are no ranks and orders, but cooperating elements, each element with its own privileges, responsibilities, and duties in seeing that the Ark goes on its way. The course of the Church is not set by cold and dead laws, but by a "Rudder" (as the collection of Canons is called in the Orthodox Church), which serves to steer it away from danger and to insure its course.

The Fathers before us, who learned their techniques of spiritual navigation from the Apostles themselves, charted our course as it was revealed to them in an unbroken chain of tradition tracing back to the Great Navigator Himself, Jesus Christ. Thus it is that we follow their course in detail, not out of blind obedience to antiquated traditions, but out of a practical understanding of the tools which they have given us. Authority is not something which allows us to act as we wish. Authority is the real power passed down to us, understood within the context of the very function of the Church, the very navigation of the Ark of Salvation. We follow the directions given to us because our actual techniques of navigation are learned from those who give those directions. That is, our skills as Christians, our sense of what it is to live the Christian life, cannot be separated from the authority of the Church. The two things operate hand-in-hand, as one. The Church functions because it has authority; the Ark is directed on a certain course because it *has* a certain course. The act of navigation contains within it a knowledge of the destination of the ship. This is the real nature of authority in the Orthodox Church.

In a practical sense, the Orthodox Church can easily establish its claim that it constitutes the Church of Christ, of the Apostles. The Church began in Jerusalem. To this day, the oldest Christian presence in Jerusalem is Orthodox. The oldest Church is that of the Brotherhood of the Holy Sepulchre —an Orthodox brotherhood. The traditions of the Orthodox Church are acknowledged even by the most polemical Westerners to be the oldest in Christianity. The structure of the Church outlined by St. Paul in his Epistles — the same structure preserved today in the Orthodox Church— was a structure that pre-dated the Canon of Scripture. All of the ancient Sees, including that of Rome, belonged to the Eastern Christian hegemony which is the source of the modern Orthodox Church. And while many Christians have broken away from the Orthodox Church, beginning with the non-Chalcedonian schism in the fifth century, there is still a number of Orthodox Christians, albeit ever smaller, who continue in absolute obedience to the traditions of the once undivided Church. They live within the Ark of the Church, removing themselves from the mundane, nurturing themselves on the same divine power which enlivened the Apostles and the Roman Empire. Their presence in the modern world, however disturbing and disquieting to those who would wish to challenge their witness, is yet another sign of the historical primacy of the Orthodox Church. They are living witneses of the past in our midst.

The functions of the Orthodox Church are also understood by Orthodox Christians in a way that would seem novel to a Westerner. Worship and ceremonies of the Church are not for the Orthodox Christian obligations, but privileges and natural functions. They are the external expression of the internal life of the Christian, rich in ritual, symbolism, and mystical content. The worship services are virtual interactions between the people and the divine, elevating moments of communion with the spiritual world, taking place outside time and space as well as in the world. The Mysteries of the Church (from the Eucharist to marriage to ordination) are numberless, since every act which lifts man up to his divine potential, binding him to God, is one which imparts Grace. (The practice of quantifying Grace and speaking of lesser or greater "Sacraments," and thus speaking of the Mysteries in terms of the seven Sacraments of the Western Church, is quite popular in the more "westernized" expositions of Orthodox thought. It grows out of an abuse of the apologetic attempts of the Orthodox to address the problems of the Reformation Era and is neither a healthy practice nor an adequate way of dealing with the Orthodox Mysteries.) In true Orthodox spirituality, the *natural function of the human being* is to worship, to take part in the divinely established services of the Church, while his only sense of obligation is to the secondary work of caring for his human needs. The Church is first, the world second; the Mysteries first, social functions and obligations second; the spiritual life of prime importance, the life of the world of lesser import.

In this very ecumenical age, when Orthodox thought has been vitiated by Western theologies, it is difficult for a true searcher to find the authentic Orthodoxy which we have contrasted with Western Christianity. In a true Orthodox community, the people live a life detached from the world. Their lives center on prayer, Church services (many hours in length when correctly done), and a simple way of life. They dress in a modest fashion. They encourage absolute moral purity. They spend more than half the year fasting from meat, fish, and dairy products (including almost every Wednesday and Friday, as well as Monday in monasteries). Married couples observe these fasts by abstention from the flesh and the cultivation of the higher aspects of marital union. Traditional Orthodox Christians stand in Church, and their Churches have no organs or musical instruments. They do not dance and engage in worldly partying in their Churches. Their Priests, giving the people images of the Prophets, the Fathers, and the spiritual world, dress at all times in long robes and refrain from cutting their hair and beards. Married Priests rear their children for service to the Church. The virgin life of monastics is exalted as the highest form of life, set aside for those who are especially gifted with moral uprightness and spiritual zeal —the strong in spirit. Such is the true Orthodox community. In it, there shines a sometimes deceptively dim light that contains a non-worldly brightness. To the outside world this life is often gloomy and dark. But those in it evidence a sad nostalgia for the spiritual world and a patient, enduring joy that is not akin to the plastic and boisterous exuberance of the emotions. Their joy is thus little understood by the modern world.

In America, this mosaic of Orthodox life barely exists. Among some of the more traditional communities, usually marked by their use of the Old (Julian) Calendar (which has been abandoned for the calendar of Pope Gregory by the majority of Orthodox in America), a traditional Orthodox spirit survives. But even many of these so-called "Old Calendarists" have lost a sense of the unity of traditions —of which the calendar is but one element— that forms genuine Orthodoxy, and there can be found the most modern of practices among them. Moreover, among Orthodox modernists, a sense of renovationism is developing, sometimes expressed in vile and almost blasphemous condemnations of the traditional piety and customs of the Orthodox Church. Not even the Divine Liturgy has escaped the vilification of some of these extremists, who condemn it as an antiquated, contrived, and senseless artifact void of the divine direction that we traditionalists impute to it. And finally, many modernist Orthodox in America, a minority of the Orthodox Faithful worldwide, have simply declared Orthodox traditionalists un-Orthodox, outside the Church, and unworthy of note.

The simple fact is that most of these modernists, infected with the excesses of ecumenism —an unfortunate movement which has, in the name of tolerance, taught them hatred for their traditionalist Orthodox brothers—, do not even honor the traditions of the Orthodox Church. They have fallen to identifying with and imitating the West. They see nothing of the uniqueness of Orthodoxy, of its singular stand as the criterion of truth, and thus find the isolation of the traditional Orthodox world ludicrous and absurd. The "peculiar" people of God they would make "mainstream." They compromise their own witness as representatives of the standard of truth, giving themselves over to distortion, rather than offering to the distorted an image of clarity and correction. Failing to see the Church as a mosaic made up of many elements, some large and some small, they dispense with this or that tradition as insignificant, not truly "ancient," or silly. They naively toss aside the traditional dress of the clergy, the rules for fasting, or the calendar which has always guided the Orthodox Church's calculation of feasts (until a reform sixty years ago in several national Churches). Picking away piece after piece of tradition, they have spoiled the image of the Church. And being unable to grasp it, they have turned to the idols of the world —some moving straightway into neo-Papism, either by moves to join with Rome or by creating in the Patriarchate of Constantinople a kind of "Eastern Papacy." Abandoning the spirit of Orthodox tradition, they have lost the very notion of the Church, its authority, and its mission as we have tried to portray them. They have lost that Eastern character which is universal to true Christians, Eastern or Western —that character which transcends geography.

All that we have written in conclusion we offer without animosity. We wish to guide those who, outside the Orthodox Church, may be confused by the spirit of modernism that assails her; at the same time, we want to emphasize to our less traditional Orthodox brothers that they have misunderstood the chasm that separates Orthodoxy from the Christianity of the West. If the Orthodox Church has preserved intact the Church of the Apostles, then those within the Church who have departed from her traditions must recapture these traditions, just as those outside the Orthodox Church must embrace them. In this return to the criterion of an authentic Faith, Orthodox and non-Orthodox have a common task —they are joined in a unity of spirit and effort. Their common discovery, indeed, is that which eventually bridges the chasm between East and West, bringing the East to what it should be and the West to what it once was. In this lies for us traditional Orthodox the ultimate Christian witness of brotherhood and love.